BALLROOM DANCING
FOR FUN!

By Jennifer Blizin Gillis

Content Adviser: Ken Richards, Vice President, DanceSport, Wilmington, Delaware
Reading Adviser: Frances J. Bonacci, Ed.D, Reading Specialist, Cambridge, Massachusetts

Compass Point Books ✦ Minneapolis, Minnesota

Compass Point Books
3109 West 50th Street, #115
Minneapolis, MN 55410

Visit Compass Point Books on the Internet at www.compasspointbooks.com
or e-mail your request to custserv@compasspointbooks.com

Photographs ©: Carson Zullinger, front cover (left), 9, 11, 16–17, 19, 24, 44 (top), 45, 47; iStockphoto, front cover (right); Sheila Burnett/Topfoto, 5, 38–39; Roger-Viollet/
Topfoto, 7, 42; Dimitrii Sherman/BigStockPhoto, 8; Kenneth C. Zirkel/iStockphoto, 10, 44 (bottom); New Line Product/Topfoto, 12–13; Bonita Cheshier/BigStockPhoto,
13 (right); Kit Sen Chin/BigStockPhoto, 14; Oleg Kozlov/BigStockPhoto, 15; Anness Publishing, 18, 22, 28, 30; Karl Schoendorfer/Rex Features, 20–21; Paul Piebinga/
iStockphoto, 26; Sipa Press/Rex Features, 32; Jeanette Jones/Rex Features, 34–35, 36–37; Tamas Szafko/stock.xchng, 38 (left); Ronald Grant Archive/Topfoto, 40; New
Line Product/Topfoto, 41; Topham Picturepoint/Topfoto, 43 (left); Miodrag Gajic/BigStockPhoto, 43 (right).

Illustrator: Jon Davis
Editors: Lionel Bender and Brenda Haugen
Designer: Bill SMITH STUDIO
Page Production: Ben White and Ashlee Schultz
Photo Researcher: Suzanne O'Farrell
Art Director: Jaime Martens
Creative Director: Keith Griffin
Editorial Director: Nick Healy
Managing Editor: Catherine Neitge
Ballroom Dancing for Fun! was produced for Compass Point Books by Bender Richardson White, UK

*The author wishes to thank Tom Tucker, president, Triangle Ballroom Dance Association,
for his expertise in the preparation of this book.*

Library of Congress Cataloging-in-Publication Data
Gillis, Jennifer Blizin, 1950-
  Ballroom dancing for fun! / by Jennifer Blizin Gillis.
    p. cm. — Includes index.
  ISBN-13: 978-0-7565-3285-7 (library binding)
  ISBN-10: 0-7565-3285-X (library binding)
1. Ballroom dancing—Juvenile literature. I. Title.
  GV1751.G465 2008
  793.3'3—dc22

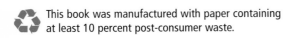

This book was manufactured with paper containing
at least 10 percent post-consumer waste.

Table of Contents

The Basics

Doing It

People, Places, and Fun

Note: In this book, there are two kinds of vocabulary words. Ballroom Words to Know are words specific to ballroom dancing. They are defined on page 46. Other Words to Know are helpful words that aren't related only to ballroom dancing. They are defined on page 47.

Light on Their Feet

Maybe you've seen dancers gliding across the floor at a party or wedding. Perhaps you've been glued to your television as dancing partners dazzle audiences with their fancy footwork. Whether it's at a party, on TV, or in the movies, ballroom dancers are fun to watch.

Good ballroom dancers make dancing look easy, but it takes lots of training and effort to become an expert. Some competitive dancers move to ballroom dance from other sports or arts, such as figure skating or ballet. Others begin taking lessons as adults and discover a talent they never knew they had!

Whether you want to dance competitively or just for fun, this book will introduce you to the basics of ballroom dance. It will show the moves and steps. It will tell you the different styles, where to learn, and how to get started. Then, with a little practice, you can take to the dance floor with style.

Vernon and Irene Castle

In the early 1900s this couple made ballroom dancing popular with their nightclub act and Broadway shows. They turned the fox-trot into one of the best-known dances of all time. They also founded a ballroom dancing school, wrote books, and made movies that taught ordinary people how to dance, dress, and behave.

From Castles to Dance Halls

Ballroom dancing got its start during a period of history called the Renaissance that lasted from about 1300 until the end of the 1500s. The kings and queens of Europe held balls at which dancers usually moved in a large circle or in two lines. Partners rarely touched each other.

In the late 1800s a growing number of public ballrooms and dance halls allowed working men and women to spend their spare time dancing.

Soon polite men and women were expected to know the steps to formal dances such as the quadrille and the minuet. The wealthiest people had ballrooms in their homes, entertained with fancy balls, and hired live-in "dancing masters."

After the American and French revolutions of the late 1700s, dances based on steps that farmers and workers had been doing for years became popular. These dances were livelier and there was more contact between partners.

"Dirty Dancing"

The waltz is the oldest ballroom dance. It was introduced in Europe in the 1800s. The newspapers and officials of the church objected to it because men and women held each other closely. This only made it more popular with young people, who could learn the three basic steps even without lessons. By the 1900s, the waltz was certainly the most popular dance in both the ballrooms of the well-to-do and working-class dance halls.

Ballroom Dancing

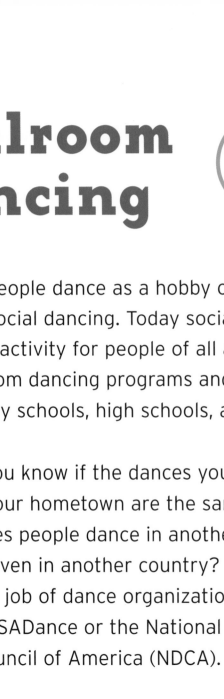

When people dance as a hobby or for fun, it is called social dancing. Today social dancing is a popular activity for people of all ages. There are ballroom dancing programs and clubs in elementary schools, high schools, and colleges.

How do you know if the dances you learn in your hometown are the same as the ones people dance in another state, or even in another country? That's the job of dance organizations such as USADance or the National Dance Council of America (NDCA).

Over the years, groups such as these have worked to standardize dance styles and steps. This means that all dances fall into certain styles, and within those styles there are certain steps. Dance organizations also help organize dances and set standards.

Dance Styles for Competitions

There are two styles of competitive ballroom dancing: American and International. American-style dance is less formal and more theatrical, allowing dance partners to break apart to perform individual steps. In International-style, dance partners remain facing each other only for standard dances.

Style	Category	Dances
American	Smooth	Waltz, Viennese waltz, tango, fox-trot
	Rhythm	Cha-cha, rumba, samba, East Coast swing, bolero, mambo
International	Standard	Waltz, Viennese waltz, tango, fox-trot, quickstep
	Latin	Cha-cha, samba, rumba, paso doble, jive

Competition

Competitive ballroom dancing is also called DanceSport. This is the type of dancing you see on television shows in which judges award points to couples based on their performances. The International DanceSport Federation, or IDSF, sets the rules for DanceSport.

Dancing partners usually specialize in a certain dance style, such as Latin or smooth, and must pass different tests to compete at a certain level. Levels may have names such as rising stars, bronze, silver, and gold. Each dance is made up of a series of standardized movements and steps.

Competitive dancers' facial expressions and attitudes are as important as their footwork. The dancers must seem sure of themselves and show a lot of energy. If they make a mistake, they must get back in step quickly and carry on with the rest of the routine.

Competitions

Competitions are made up of heats, a series of dances designed to eliminate dancers from the competition. Only 12 couples go on to the semifinals. Six of these couples go on to the finals, from which the winners are chosen.

11

First Steps

It's easy to find a ballroom dancing class. Chain studios, such as Arthur Murray and Fred Astaire Studios, offer classes to people of all ages, all over the world. Or check with your local parks and recreation department or community college to find classes.

When you are looking for ballroom classes, ask questions, such as: Is the instructor certified? A certified instructor teaches standardized steps and uses teaching methods approved by the National Dance Council of America. How many students will be in your class? The larger the class, the less attention your instructor will be able to give you. Private lessons may be more expensive.

Talk to the instructors. Do they seem friendly and patient? An instructor should be genuinely interested in your progress and not just see teaching as a way of making money. Finally, if you think you want to dance competitively, you will want an instructor who competes or who is familiar with DanceSport.

Homework

Plan to spend time at home practicing what you learned in class. It is easier and more realistic to practice for 10 or 15 minutes twice every day than to try to set aside a whole hour or more once a week.

What to Wear

Shoes are a ballroom dancer's most important piece of equipment. Professional ballroom dancing shoes are leather with suede soles, sometimes called chrome leather soles.

Although you shouldn't need special ballroom shoes for your first few lessons, it's important to wear flexible shoes with a thin sole. This allows your foot to feel the dance floor. Athletic shoes drag on the floor and keep your feet from moving freely and smoothly. Make sure your shoes will stay on your feet no matter what! Shoes that tie or have straps are best. If you have to buy a pair of shoes but don't want to spend a lot, try bowling shoes. They are as comfortable as athletic shoes and are flexible enough to allow you to move well.

Shoes for Latin and rhythm dances have straps so they can't fly off.

Women's professional ballroom shoes have heels and rounded or open toes. Lace-up leather shoes are standard footwear for male professional ballroom dancers.

Wear close-fitting clothes that let you move easily and allow the instructor to clearly see your movements.

At social dances and for competitions, women wear dresses or skirts while men wear dress pants and shirts with jackets and ties. But during class, comfort is the key.

Beware of baggy pants and swirling skirts that can get tangled with your partner's legs and cause embarrassing trips or falls.

Warming Up

A good warm-up can prevent soreness or injury. Dancers usually begin at the head and work down the body as they warm up. Breathe deeply; keep your shoulders down, your stomach in, and your knees loose.

Head Rolls

Stand with your feet apart. Gently drop your head forward until your chin nearly touches your chest. Hold this position for 30 seconds. Then slowly roll your head toward your right shoulder. Roll your head back to the center, then toward your left shoulder. Repeat five times.

Shoulder Rolls

Keep your feet slightly apart. Roll your right shoulder back, down, and under as if you were drawing a circle with it. Repeat two or three times. Then do the same exercise with your left shoulder. Finish by rolling both shoulders at the same time.

Hip Circles

With your feet still slightly apart, place your hands on your hips. Move your hips to the right, then the back, then to the left, and back to the front as if you are drawing a circle with your body. Repeat several times. Then move your hips left, then to the back, then the front as if making a circle in the opposite direction.

Ankle Circles

Sit with your back against a wall, legs extended in front of you. Lift your right leg slightly off the floor, and make small circles with your ankle, first in one direction and then the other. Put your right leg down, and repeat the exercise with your left leg.

Position

In ballroom dancing, one partner, usually the man, leads, and the other follows. For much or all of the dance, the leader is stepping forward while the follower is stepping backward. Most dances begin with leaders stepping forward on their left feet as followers step backward on their right feet.

Most social dancing is done in the closed position, with partners facing each other. Although photos may seem to show partners standing toe to toe, the follower really stands slightly to the right of the leader's feet. As the partners move, the leader's right foot is pointing between the follower's feet. In some dances, such as the tango, the partners may stand so that they connect more on their left sides.

1. In the closed position, both partners stand with heads up and stomachs held in.

2. Partners look out over each other's right shoulder.

3. The leader places his right hand on the follower's back, just below the left shoulder blade.

4. The follower lightly rests her left arm on top of the leader's right arm with the fingers of her left hand on his shoulder.

5. The leader lightly holds the follower's right hand in his left hand at about the height of the woman's ear.

6. Both the man's and the woman's elbows are raised, but their shoulders stay down.

Dancing Distance

In American-style dance, couples stand 3 to 6 inches (7.5 to 15 cm) apart for most dances.

Do's and Don'ts

There is an etiquette, or group of rules that everyone agrees on, for social dancing. Following these rules helps dancers have a good time.

DO:

- Bathe or shower, and brush your teeth. You will be very close to your partner.

- Hold your partner lightly.

- Follow your leader even if you don't like the way he is doing a dance.

- Dance with different partners.

- Apologize for any mistakes, such as stepping on your partner's feet or missing a step.

- Be aware of others on the dance floor, and avoid banging into them.

Always

Thank your partner at the end of the dance, and leave the dance floor promptly.

DON'T:

- Wear athletic shoes. They can cause injuries to your ankles or knees.

- Push or pull your partner around.

- Scold your partner if he or she makes a mistake.

- Hog the dance floor or try to show off.

- Refuse a dance with someone and then dance with a different partner.

- Say yes to dancing with someone if you don't know the dance. Instead say, "I'd like to, but I don't know this dance. Would you mind showing me?"

The Waltz

The waltz is the most basic ballroom dance. It is a traveling, or progressive, dance, meaning that couples move around the floor counter-clockwise as they dance. If you listen to a waltz tune, you will hear this rhythm—ONE, two, three; ONE, two, three. Another way to think of it is quick, quick, quick.

The steps you and your partner take will make a box shape. Begin this dance from the closed position, with your feet together. The steps to the side are made on the balls of the feet, so that the dance has a rising and falling motion.

LEADER

1. Step forward with your left foot.
2. Bring your right foot forward, then out to the right side, stepping on the ball of your right foot.
3. Bring your left foot close to your right foot.
4. Step back on your right foot.
5. Bring your left foot back then out to the side, stepping on the ball of your left foot.
6. Bring your right foot close to your left foot.

The Closed Position

Begin this and many of the other dances from the closed position.

FOLLOWER

1. Step backward with your right foot.
2. Move your left leg backward, then out to the left side, stepping on the ball of your left foot.
3. Bring your right foot close to your left.
4. Step forward on your left foot.
5. Bring your right foot out to the side, stepping on the ball of your right foot.
6. Bring your left foot close to your right foot.

The Fox-trot

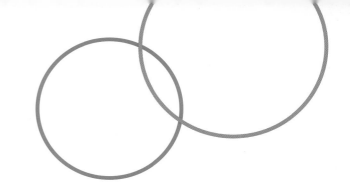

The fox-trot is another traveling, or progressive, dance. It gets its name from Harry Fox, an actor who made the dance popular in the early 1900s. The rhythm of this dance is slow, slow, quick, quick. Your feet stay on the floor for the slow steps, while you take the quick steps on the balls of your feet. This gives the fox-trot a rising and falling movement.

In competition, ballroom dancers must have lots of attitude.

LEADER

1. (Slow) Step forward on your left foot.
2. (Slow) Move your right foot forward.
3. (Quick) Move your left foot to the side and slightly forward.
4. (Quick) Close your right foot to your left foot.

FOLLOWER

1. Step back on your right foot.
2. Move your left foot backward.
3. Move your right foot to the side and slightly forward.
4. Close your left foot to your right foot.

Begin in the closed position.

The Tango

The tango is a traveling dance that got its start in Argentina. Its dramatic style and quick head turns make the tango one of the most popular ballroom dances.

To learn the tango walk, think of a cat sneaking up on something. It takes a few slow steps, then pounces. Tango partners stand in closed position very close to each other with their bodies facing slightly to the left. Partners' bodies touch at the leader's left hip and the follower's right hip. In some cases, the leader's knees go between the follower's legs as they step. The leader's arm goes far around the follower's body, with his fingers resting on her spine. Both partners take the slow steps with their knees flexed.

LEADER

1. Take a giant step forward on your left leg, knees bent.
2. Take a giant step forward on your right leg, knees bent.
3. Take a small, quick step forward on your left leg.
4. Move your right foot to the side, toes first. Then set your right heel down.
5. Bring your left foot close to your right foot.

The rhythm of the tango is slow, slow, quick, quick, slow. Another way to remember the rhythm is T ... A ... N, G, O.

FOLLOWER

1. Take a giant step backward on your right leg.
2. Take a giant step backward on your left foot.
3. Take a small, quick step backward on your right leg.
4. Move your left foot to the side, toes first. Then set your left heel down.
5. Bring your right foot close to your left foot.

The Rumba

The rumba is a Latin, or rhythm, dance. There is a rocking hip motion, called "Cuban Motion," which comes from the dancer's flexed knees.

During the rumba, the dancers bring the ball of each foot forward first, pressing toward the floor as they move. Think of climbing a ladder. You step with the ball of your right foot, knee bent, on the first rung. Then you bend your left knee and step with the ball of your left foot on the next rung, and so on. Put this in a sequence, and you have the dance.

LEADER

1. Step forward on your left foot, knees flexed, ball of the foot first.

2. Move your right foot to the side.

3. Bring your left foot close to your right foot.

4. Step back on your right foot.

5. Move your left foot to the side.

6. Bring your right foot close to your left foot.

FOLLOWER

1. Step back on your right foot, knees flexed, ball of the foot first.

2. Move your left foot to the side.

3. Bring your right foot close to your left foot.

4. Step forward on your left foot.

5. Move your right foot to the side.

6. Bring your left foot close to your right foot.

This is an American-style box step. Start in closed position, with 3 to 6 inches (7.5 to 15 cm) between you and your partner. The rhythm for this dance is slow, quick, quick.

The Cha-cha

The cha-cha is also a Latin, or rhythm, dance. It is a "spot" dance, meaning that the dancers stay in the same place instead of traveling around the dance floor.

Cha-cha music is lively and energetic. The rhythm of this dance is one, two, three, four AND one, two, three, four. It is really a chassé in which dancers step quickly from the right foot to the left foot and back to the right foot again.

LEADER

Begin with your right foot pointing to the side. (Your weight is on your left foot.)

1. Shift your weight to your right foot.

2. Step forward on your left foot.

3. Shift your weight to your right foot.

4 & 1. Chassé left, right, left.

2. Step back on your right foot.

3. Shift your weight to your left foot.

4 & 1. Chassé right, left, right.

FOLLOWER

Begin with your left foot pointing to the side. (If dancing side-to-side, as in the photo, follow the leader's footsteps.)

1. Shift your weight to your left foot.

2. Step backward on your right foot.

3. Shift your weight to your left foot.

4 & 1. Chassé right, left, right.

2. Step forward on your left foot.

3. Shift your weight to your right foot.

4 & 1. Chassé left, right, left.

East Coast Swing

Swing is a basic social dance with different styles. Country Western or cowboy swing, the shag, West Coast swing, East Coast swing, and jive are different versions of swing.

Couples begin facing each other, holding hands with their arms slightly bent and relaxed. Swing can also be danced in the closed position. Swing has a six-count rhythm—one and two, three and four, five, six. The chassés are made quickly.

LEADER

1. Chassé left: step left, right, left.
2. Chassé right: step right, left, right.
3. Step back on your left foot.
4. Shift your weight to your right foot.

FOLLOWER

1. Chassé left: step right, left, right.
2. Chassé right: step left, right, left.
3. Step back on your right foot.
4. Shift your weight to your left foot.

Exclusively American

There are International-style and American-style versions of the waltz, fox-trot, tango, rumba, and cha-cha. East Coast swing is strictly an American-style dance. In International-style competitions, jive takes the place of East Coast swing.

Dance Around the World

Since the 1940s, ballroom dancing has been popular as a form of entertainment and recreation in the United States, Great Britain, and Australia.

You may notice that many ballroom champions have Eastern European or Russian names. A long tradition of dance in countries such as Russia, Poland, and Ukraine has created a great interest in ballroom dancing. It is serious business in communities with large populations of immigrants from Eastern Europe.

In Asia, ballroom dancing is an absolute craze, especially among older people.

In 1996, *Shall We Dance*, a Japanese movie about a businessman who changed his boring life by taking dance lessons, brought a new interest in social dance to Japan. In the Philippines, many discos and bars have become ballroom dance businesses, and one of the fastest-growing careers is that of dance instructor.

According to the Chinese DanceSport Federation, more than 30 million people in China participate in ballroom dancing programs. Although there are plenty of private clubs and indoor ballrooms, many people prefer to dance outdoors in public parks.

The Blackpool Dance Festival

The oldest and most well-known competition is the Blackpool Dance Festival in Great Britain. Each year, dancers ages 6 years and older come from all over the world to compete in several categories.

Ballroom Heroes

Elena Kryuchkova tried ice skating and gymnastics before she discovered her passion for ballroom dancing at the age of 9. Later she met Andrei Gavrilene, a Moscow law student who also loved to dance. In 1999 they moved to the United States and got married. Two years later they became the Rising Star Latin Dance Champions at the Blackpool Dance Festival in Great Britain. They are two-time U.S. National Professional Latin Dance champions and have represented the United States in the World Latin American Dance Championships.

Champion ballroom dancers compete at the Royal Albert Hall in England.

Valentin Chmerkovskiy is famous for his spins. He can perform eight spins in two seconds! At the age of 16, Valentin and his former partner, Diana Olonetskaya, were the first Americans ever to win a world junior championship dance competition. When Valentin and his family arrived in New York from Ukraine, it was his older brother Max who was the rising star. Their father started a dance studio so that Max could continue training. However, though Max is one of seven top Latin dancers in the world, the spotlight is now on Valentin. At 20, Valentin is probably the best American Latin dancer in the world.

Olympic Hopes

There is one major difference between competitive ballroom dancing and ice dancing or rhythmic gymnastics. Competitive ballroom dancing—known as DanceSport—is not yet an Olympic event.

DanceSport

DanceSport competitors have participated in the Olympics but only as entertainers. At the 2000 Olympics in Sydney, Australia, U.S. champions David and Sharon Savoy performed an exhibition dance. Australian champions Jason Gilkison and Peta Roby performed a mambo in the closing ceremonies.

For many years the International DanceSport Federation has worked to have DanceSport included in an Olympic program. In 1997 the International Olympic Committee recognized DanceSport as an athletic event and approved the IDSF to represent the sport. That same year, DanceSport was included in the program of the fifth Annual World Games. DanceSport has been included as an event in the Asian Games since 1998. It was added to the World Games in Japan in 2001 and is also included in the East Asian Games.

On the Screen

In the 1930s and 1940s the dance team of Fred Astaire and Ginger Rogers inspired movie audiences with their dazzling ballroom style. American-style ballroom dance is based on their act. Movies made ballroom dancing a popular pastime, and there were supper clubs, nightclubs, and public ballrooms where people danced like the stars of the silver screen.

Popular movies often included dance routines well into the 1950s. The disco hero in *Saturday Night Fever* brought everyday people back to dance studios in the late 1970s to learn the latest disco steps.

Today ballroom dancing is back, and there are a number of movies to prove it. In the early 1990s *Strictly Ballroom*, an Australian movie, told the story of a ballroom champion who chose an unlikely dance partner.

Antonio Banderas starred in *Take the Lead*, a movie based on the school dance program shown in the 2005 documentary *Mad Hot Ballroom*.

What Happened When?

| 1500 | 1800 | 1900 | 1910 | 1920 |

1500s Formal dances become popular in the royal courts of Europe.

1808 The Apollo, a dance hall said to hold 6,000 dancers at a time, opens in Vienna, Austria.

1909 The first world championship dance competition is held in Paris, France.

1812 The German waltz is introduced in England.

1910 The first public exhibition of the tango takes place in Paris.

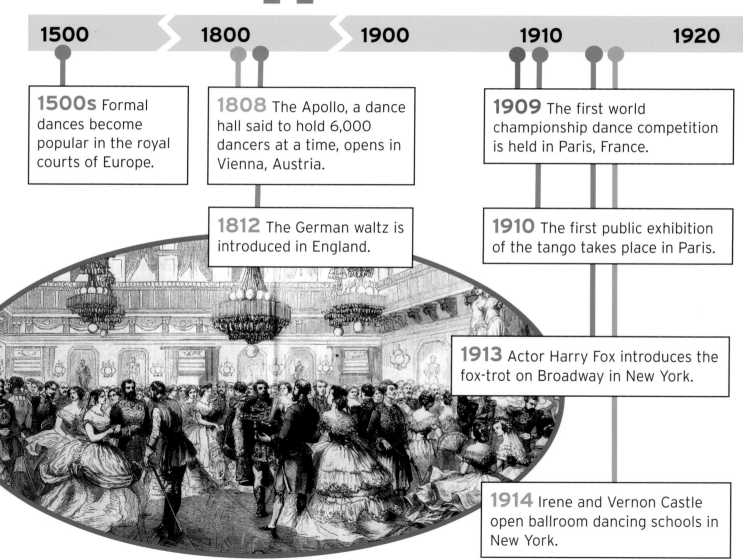

1913 Actor Harry Fox introduces the fox-trot on Broadway in New York.

1914 Irene and Vernon Castle open ballroom dancing schools in New York.

1930　　1940　　1950　　1960　　1970　　1980　　1990　　2000

1930s Movies such as *Top Hat* and *Flying Down to Rio* help create American-style ballroom dance.

1948 The National Dance Council of America is formed.

1950 The International Council of Ballroom Dancing (today known as the World Dance and DanceSport Council) is formed.

1965 The United States Amateur Ballroom Dancing Association (today known as USADance) is formed.

1997 The International Olympic Committee recognizes DanceSport as an official sport.

2004 In Britain, the BBC relaunches its 1949 pioneering *Come Dancing* program with celebrity dancers.

Fun Ballroom Facts

Ballroom dance is more than just fun; it's also good for you. Studies have shown that moderate ballroom dancing, such as waltzing and fox-trotting, can burn between 250 and 300 calories an hour.

The movie *Take the Lead* is based on the true story of Pierre Dulain, who started ballroom dancing programs in New York City Public Schools in the 1990s. More than 12,000 students have participated.

The tango was originally danced by Argentine cowboys and dance-hall girls. The cowboys came to the dance halls wearing clothes they wore on the job. The dance-hall girls held their heads back to cut down on the smell of horses and cows coming from their partners!

Female DanceSport competitors rarely wear black for smooth or standard dances. Since male competitors wear black in competitions, judges would have difficulty seeing the difference between the man's and the woman's movements.

Ballroom Words to Know

box step: dance steps in which movement of the feet make an imaginary box shape

chassé: [sha-SAY] dance step made by sliding the feet or galloping to the right or left

chrome leather: leather shoe soles treated so that they are slightly rough

closed position: basic ballroom dance position in which the leader and follower stand with feet facing each other, looking over each other's shoulders. The leader holds the follower's right hand in his left, while the follower rests her left hand on the leader's right shoulder blade.

finals: last dance in a competition that decides the top winners

flexed knees: bent knees

follower: the partner who moves backward, usually the woman

heat: one of several competitions to choose the best dancers from a large group to move on to the semifinals

leader: the partner who directs the couple's movements on the dance floor, usually the man

minuet: [mihn-you-ET] very slow, formal dance that was popular in the 1600s and 1700s

progressive dance: dance in which couples move around the dance floor, also called a traveling dance

quadrille: [kwa-DREEL] dance in which four couples face each other and perform various steps with one another

rise and fall: appearance of going up and down when dancers make some steps on flat feet and others on the balls of their feet

semifinals: competition between the winners of earlier heats to choose dancers for the finals

traveling dance: one in which couples move around the dance floor, also called a progressive dance

GLOSSARY
Other Words to Know

counter-clockwise: opposite the direction hands on a clock move

etiquette: group of rules that tell how people should behave in public

flexible: able to bend

professional: paid to do something

standardize: made widely known and accepted as correct

technique: the manner in which something is accomplished

Where to Learn More

At The Library
Silvester, Victor. *Modern Ballroom Dancing*. North Pomfret, Vt.: Trafalgar Square, 2005.

Spencer, Peggy. *The Joy of Dancing: ballroom, Latin, and rock/jive for absolute beginners of all ages.* London: Carlton, 2004.

Trautman, Shawn and Joanna Trautman. *Picture Yourself Dancing: Step-by-step instruction for ballroom, Latin, country, and more.* Boston, Mass.: Thomson Course Technology, 2006.

On The Road
National Museum of Dance and
   Hall of Fame
99 S. Broadway
Saratoga Springs, NY 12866
518/584-2225

On The Web
For more information on this topic, use FactHound.

1. Go to *www.facthound.com*
2. Type in this book ID: 075653285X
3. Click on the *Fetch It* button.

FactHound will find the best Web sites for you.

INDEX

ABOUT THE AUTHOR

Jennifer Blizin Gillis took her first ballroom dancing lessons at the age of 13. Today she is a writer and a librarian in Pittsboro, North Carolina. She still has her dancing shoes but spends most of her time writing and taking care of her two dogs and two cats.